T0195060

**"The Last Supper"** *by Gustave Doré*

Mar 14:22-24 And as they did eat, Jesus took bread, and blessed, and brake it, and gave to them, and said, Take, eat: this is my body. And he took the cup, ... This is my blood of the new testament, which is shed for many.

# Jesus Is God

## Is

### Scripture Proves It

CARY GLENN

WESTBOW
PRESS®
A DIVISION OF THOMAS NELSON
& ZONDERVAN

WestBow Press books may be ordered through booksellers or by contacting:

WestBow Press
A Division of Thomas Nelson & Zondervan
1663 Liberty Drive
Bloomington, IN 47403
www.westbowpress.com
844-714-3454

Scripture quotations marked (NLT) are taken from the Holy Bible,
New Living Translation, copyright © 1996, 2004, 2007 by Tyndale
House Foundation. Used by permission of Tyndale House Publishers,
Inc., Carol Stream, Illinois 60188. All rights reserved.

ISBN: 978-1-6642-1437-8 (sc)
ISBN: 978-1-6642-1436-1 (e)

Library of Congress Control Number: 2020923872

Print information available on the last page.

WestBow Press rev. date: 12/21/2020

# Preface

This book is about the information I found during my search for the truth in different religions and my research in the Holy Bible about Jesus the Christ being not only the Messiah and Savior but also God Almighty. I call Him Jesus our Christ or Jesus the Christ because He is the Messiah and our Savior, not Mr. Christ. Christ means Anointed One in Greek. You will hear Jesus called the Messiah, which means Anointed One in Hebrew, and the word *Saviour*, which means one who saves in British English.

I use the New Living Translation (NLT), and all biblical quotes come from this source unless otherwise stated because I found it to be a wonderful translation. It was translated from all the oldest texts available and the Dead Sea Scrolls. Unlike the King James Version, it's much easier to read. The New Living Translation is in today's English, rather than the four-hundred-year-old English that is hard to understand. We don't speak like that today. I do like to reference the King James though. I have a parallel Bible that has four versions side by side. All scriptures underneath the illustrations are from the King James Bible.

I am not any kind of scholar, professor, teacher, preacher, or learned professional on Bible scriptures. I'm not a learned theological professional either. I'm just your average, ordinary Christian searching for the truths in God's Word. First John 2:27 says that when you have the Holy Spirit in you, He will teach you the Word. You don't need anyone to teach you when the Holy Spirit is on your side.

First off, I grew up a Baptist. After my years of studies, I now simply call myself a Christian—a Christ follower and not the religion that uses the name Christian. I'm just a man who reads the Bible and follows Jesus the Christ—well, tries to anyway. I am a sinner just like the rest of the world. The Jesus who died on the cross for my sins was raised the third day and is my Lord and my God. I worship no other. I do not follow any established religion.

My parents took me to church on a regular basis. I went to vacation Bible school, played on the church softball team, and sang in the youth choir. I went on church outings and was a wiseman in the church play. My mother was a Christian schoolteacher for ten-plus years and wrote a Bible questionnaire learning game to help her students whom she took to compete against other Christian schools. She also sold quite a few of her books to the competing schools. I thank my wonderful parents, my Grandmother Margie and my Grandfather Elmo for bringing me up with a Christian education.

Once I grew up, I began to question religion. How did I know if what I grew up learning was the truth with all the different religions that are out there? Did you know that in Christianity alone, there are over thirty-three thousand denominations in 238 countries? So many different interpretations. There are so many different views within so many different religions that they all can't be true. They are not all true. Some are so far off the truth that one can only wonder how anyone could put any faith in them, and parents *can* be wrong.

I spent five years fervently studying religion itself, not just Christianity. I started off with, of course, Christianity. If I were going to believe it, then I wanted to know, to see for myself, what it really said. There are over 150 pages about the history of Christianity in the Encyclopaedia Britannica. I have read the entire Bible too many times to count. I bought books on topics from truths of the Bible, Christian history, theology, first-century historians such as Flavius Josephus, the Crusades, the popes, and so much more. I even read everything I could find on what the skeptics had to say. I wanted to know what they were saying and if they had any ground to stand on. I found that they did not. They were lacking in their understanding.

After my studies in Christianity, I investigated the Islamic religion and read the Koran multiple times. That book has a lot of the Old Testament copied straight out of the Bible—twisted around, of course. I compared what I found in the Koran to the Bible and discovered that nothing in the Koran made any sense to me and I could not find any shred of validity to substantiate the claims that it made. I found it to be full of quotes and proverbs that mirrored the Bible but taken out of context, contradicting chapters, verses that didn't make any sense, and went against known proven science. It was as if someone sat down with the Bible and scribbled out a new religion. I now know why some people who read the Koran think they need to kill the infidel—because it tells them to!

My next venture took me to Judaism. My thoughts on the Jewish people are the same as it says in scripture; they have been blinded and can only be saved by believing in Jesus. Their eyes will be opened upon His Second Coming. Christianity has its roots in the Jewish Torah, which we call the Old Testament. Christianity is just a continuation of the Jewish faith. We believe in the Jewish Messiah—Jesus. The Jews, meanwhile, think of Him as just a prophet but then believe nothing He says and are still waiting on a Messiah to come.

Next, I explored Mormonism. I studied with an acquaintance of mine who happened to be a Mormon. I found the religion to resemble a science fiction novel. They use four different books in their religion: Doctrines and Covenants, the Book of Mormon, the Pearl of Great Price, and the King James Bible that contradicts the prior three. The Book of Mormon starts out by saying that it's "another Testament from Jesus Christ." Look in scripture:

> "I am shocked that you are turning away so soon from God, … You are following a different way that pretends to be the Good News but is not the Good News at all. You are being fooled by those who deliberately twist the truth concerning Christ. Let God's curse fall on anyone, including us or even an angel from heaven, who preaches a different kind of Good News than the one we preached to you. I say again what we have said before: if anyone preaches any other Good News than the one you welcomed, let that person be cursed." (Galatians 1:6–9)

They call themselves Christians, but everything they believe is different from what the Bible preaches. Joseph Smith supposedly got information from the angel Moroni beginning in late 1823 and used seer stones to "see" the future and obtain his prophecies, yet neither early books nor his golden plates can be found. The disciples put it plainly that anyone be cursed that preaches a different message, and they wanted them to know how serious it was by reiterating the curse. Didn't we just read that even if an angel brings a different message, let him be cursed? Yeah, we did. But Mormons trust their fate to this angel Moroni. Hmm.

Mormons believe that man became God, not that God became a man. So, according to their religion, one can become the God of his own world, just like Jesus did—unless you are a woman or person of color. Sorry. The Book of Mormon mirrors the Bible more than the Koran does. Only they say, oh look, the same thing that happened in Jewish history happened to us too but here in the new world—America. To this day, no archaeological dig has *ever* unearthed a shred of evidence to corroborate their story. Did I stress *ever* enough? Mormonism has gone through so many doctrinal changes throughout its history that Joseph Smith, their so-called prophet, wouldn't even recognize the religion if he were alive today. I could go on and on about the fallacies in Mormonism, but that's a book in itself. People say that Christianity has also gone through lots of changes with Catholics and Protestants splitting over doctrinal differences. There are uncountable differences in the things that so-called Christians and true Christians have disagreed on. But *never* has the true beginning message from the disciples *ever* changed. That's the message that Jesus is the only way to salvation.

The Jehovah's Witness religion was on my list of readings too. I studied for six months with a sixty-year-old man who grew up a devout follower in that religion. He came to me when he started having serious doubts about what he was being taught. We would go to the meetings at the Kingdom Hall and then go home and pull out the Bible to see if what we found there was what they taught in their meetings. It rarely was. We were only allowed to read exactly what was printed in the pamphlets they put out, the *Watchtower*. I tried to read on to get the context of the paragraph correct and was abruptly stopped and told I couldn't go on. When I tried to question what they were preaching, they quickly and somewhat rudely shut me down and moved on. They have a story, and they would have someone read it and then someone else go to a Bible verse, pull it out of a paragraph, and make it fit their story. That's all. No more. They didn't use the verse in the context it was written but put that verse into their made-up story and say, "See, it says so in the Bible. Praise God!" It's crazy. After our studies, that man quit their religion. Glory be to the true God. I don't know where he is today. He told me how fanatically they would come after him to repent and rejoin their group. If he didn't, then he would be banned from their presence and shunned.

I found the Christian religion through the Holy Bible to be the *only* authoritative religion with *any* shred of evidence that what it is claiming is true. That authority comes in the form of the prophecies. *No other religion in the entire world has them.* There are not just a few of them. There are thousands of them that have come true and lots more to come. These prophecies are not vague or hollow like those of the French astrologer, physician, and reputed seer Nostradamus, who was born in 1503 and wrote a book called *Les Prophecies*. His book contained 942 poetic quatrains supposedly predicting future events. He himself said that only about 10 percent of his prophecies came true. You may have heard people saying he predicted the twin towers falling in New York, Hitler, and many other events in our time. I've read them. They are so vague you could put any story or event into any one of them. They say things like, some towers in a big city will burn and fall. None of them are specific like Bible prophecies that give names, dates, peoples, time frames, and specific events. One prophecy in the Bible says that the Israelites would one day come back and be a people again in their homeland. Do you know that no other conquered people in history have ever come back and became a people again? None. Look at the archaeological finds in the Middle East where the Hittites, Amorites, Kushites, Philistines, Persians, Babylonians, and so many more were conquered. The people left over after being conquered were assimilated into the conquerors' kingdoms. None of them are countries today. But in 1948 Israel became a country again, known as the State of Israel. That's specific prophecy. Ezekiel 34:8–18 is the full prophecy. The Israelites were scattered all over the Middle East and the world. They came back by the thousands to live in the ancient lands of Israel in 1948.

"For this is what the Sovereign LORD says: I myself will search and find my sheep. I will be like a shepherd looking for his scattered flock. I will find my sheep and rescue them from all the places where they were scattered on that dark and cloudy day. I will bring them back home to their own land of Israel from among the peoples and nations..." (Ezekiel 34:11–13)

As you read these passages, read them with the thought that you believe that Jesus was and is God. He is where the entire Bible points. It's all one continuous, unchanging story about our God and how He wants to save us. He gave us His Holy Word and made sure it was passed down through the centuries just as it was first copied down. The God I believe in is powerful enough to ensure that His word remains the same throughout the ages or humankind is doomed. Make sure that you go to each verse I point out. That's why I put them right there in the paragraphs and not in notes at the end of the pages or back of the book. It's especially important that you do so that you will see the meaning I'm showing in scripture.

I hope you enjoy this book, retain some of this information, and continue in your own studies of scripture. God bless you as you read.

**"Destruction of the Army of the Amorites"** *by Gustave Doré*

Jos 10:11 ...the Lord cast down great stones from heaven upon them unto Azekah, and they died: *they were* more which died with hailstones than *they* whom the children of Israel slew with the sword.

# Jesus's Statement to Humankind

Before you begin reading this book, start out with a prayer to God, the God of Isaac, Abraham, Jacob, and Moses. Ask Him to reveal His message to you. Ask Him to open your eyes to His true Word. Take what you are reading at face value. There are no hidden meanings, no codes, and truly no secret script. There is just the true Word of God that will give you the knowledge that you need to gain the gift of salvation that God gives to us. It is not earned; it's a gift (Romans 5).

Throughout this book, you will read passages that either say that Jesus is God, imply that He is God, or leave you with the feeling that He is God. Do not read too much into the passages or try and place meaning in there that just isn't present. Make sure that you go to each verse that I point out and read not just the verse but the entire paragraph to ensure that you see the meaning that the prophets were writing. That is when you will get the proper interpretation of what you are reading. You can put any meaning into a single sentence, especially when you pull it out of the paragraph it's written in and place it in a totally new one. The prophets wrote these verses with a specific meaning in each paragraph. You must read the sentence in its proper context as the prophet was using it, not what someone else tells you it means by itself, like the Jehovah's Witnesses do.

Jesus made an extremely important statement in John 8:24 that lets us know one imperative aspect of what we need to believe for our salvation. He said, "For unless you believe that I AM who I claim to be, you will die in your sins." Jesus told us to believe that He is God, or we will die in our sins. That means that if we don't believe that He is God, we will go to hell. It's that simple and, luckily, that easy. All we must do is genuinely believe in our hearts. Throughout scripture, Jesus is either insinuating or saying that He is our God, and it's extremely important that we honestly believe that in our hearts. And God knows what we genuinely believe. If we do not, then it's to our own destruction.

# Don't Miss the Point When Reading Scripture

There are so many different interpretations of the Bible in the world today; how can I know which one is true? How do I know what is right? Who should I listen to? I'm not smart enough to read for myself and determine what is truly being said. It's all so confusing. Does this sound like you when you are reading anything? You don't have to be a scholar to read the Bible. No. You do not. You must take what you are reading in the context in which it's written, and that's not hard to do. When someone writes a paragraph, there is a topic and a certain meaning the author is trying to convey to the reader. So many people out there want to take one or two sentences out of a paragraph and put it into their story and claim the Bible backs up their story.

Here are some quick points a lot of people miss when they sit down to read scripture:

- Read the verse in its proper rendering.

- How is it written?

- To whom is it written?

- Who is speaking?

- What is the point of the entire paragraph?

A passage in John 6:50–60 says that if you don't eat my flesh and drink my blood, you cannot get into heaven. Wow! Lunchtime. Taken way out of context, you would think that a Christian had to be a vampire and drink human blood like Count Dracula to get into heaven. Here is the verse:

> "But anyone who eats my flesh and drinks my blood has eternal life, and I will raise that person at the last day." (John 6:54)

When you read this paragraph in its proper context, you will understand that Jesus is speaking of the Word of God. He is saying to take His message deep into your hearts and live the Word. He is speaking of living a Christian life and zealously following His teachings, not turning into a bat, flying around in the moonlight, and preying on helpless victims for a bloody midnight snack. Yummy. Doesn't that sound tasty?

When you just look at the one verse pulled out of the paragraph, you can put it into countless scenarios. You can make up any story you want with any meaning, like so many people out there are doing every day and passing it on as truth. But is it the meaning that the original author of that paragraph intended for you to read? Did Jesus really want you to become a cannibal and eat His flesh and drink His blood? Of course not. He wanted passion in following His Word.

## "Baruch Writing Jeremiah's Prophecies" *by Gustave Doré*

Jer 36:4 Then Jeremiah called Baruch the son of Neriah: and Baruch wrote from the mouth of Jeremiah all the words of the Lord, which he had spoken unto him, upon a roll of a book.

# Believability of the Bible

The Bible in its entirety is to be believed. You can't believe the parts of the Bible that sound good or the parts that fit into your lifestyle and then cast off the rest of it that doesn't fit because you don't like what it says. If only parts of it are truthful, then how can any of it be believed? The Bible is an all-or-nothing deal. There are so many religions that compare themselves to Christianity and use parts of its scriptures way out of context to make their made-up stories sound true and authoritative. Biblical archaeology in the Middle East around Israel and its surrounding lands uncover more and more evidence every year that proves the stories in the Bible true. In all history, never has a story from the Bible been proven wrong. But over and over, archaeological discoveries are continuing to prove the stories to be true.

Unlike *all* other religions in the world, Christianity offers the reader what none of them can. Proof. That's right. Pure and simple proof. It's proof that what it is claiming is and will come true exactly as it was written. You ask, "How can you prove that?" You can prove it by the Bible being believable in *everything* it says. The Bible offers you proof and makes it believable through the events predicted in the prophecies. You say many people have predicted future events throughout history. Yes. You are correct. Many people have made predictions that have come true throughout the centuries. These same so-called prophets have also made many predictions that did not come to fruition, but none have been able to write thousands of specific predictions of future events and have had every one of them come true exactly as they were written as the Bible prophets have. Not vague speech but precise writings known as the prophecies.

The Old Testament is over fifteen hundred years of Jewish history that you can find recorded in biblical and secular texts. A written history can be referenced to validate these prophecies. In some cases, hundreds of years separated the prophets from the time when their prophecies came true so that anyone alive at the time would not be accused of trying to make these predictions come true. Without this historical record, there would be no way to know when and what was predicted. It is there for you to research and see for yourself that the Christian Bible is the only religion in the world today that can offer its followers proof of its legitimacy. This knowledge should give you the presence of mind to delve into the Bible wholeheartedly and without any hesitation to believe what is written.

# Precursor for Father, Son, and Holy Ghost

*H*ere are some passages where you really should pay close attention to what and how something is written. Look at the very beginning of human existence. Genesis 1:26 says, "Then God said, 'Let *us* make man in *our* image, to *our* likeness'" (emphases added). God is the one speaking, and He uses the words *us* and *our*. These are plural terms meaning more than one. So many people read that passage and say, "Look, there are many gods." That's just not the case. Read the next verse and pay close attention to how it is written. Genesis 1:27 goes on to say, "So God created human beings in *his* own image. In the image of God *he* created *them*; male and female created *he them*." (emphases added). Here, scripture uses the singular form of the word when speaking of the image that humans were created in: His. Then it goes on to say, "his own," but in the verse just before this one God says let's create man in "our" image. God is telling humans right there that the Father, the Son, and the Holy Ghost

9

are one. It's a precursor to what we see later in scripture. Humans are made in the image of God, and Jesus is that very image. The last part of verse 27 lets you know that they knew the plural form from singular when it says, "Male and female created *he* [God] *them* [male and female]."

> "Christ is the visible image of the invisible God…"
> (Colossians 1:15)

There are more instances of the singular pronoun in Revelation 22:1–6. Verse 1 says a river flows "from the throne of God and the Lamb". Again, proper English would use the plural word *thrones* if they were two. It names one throne but gives the two names of God and the Lamb.

Look at verse 3; it is even clearer. It says, "No longer will there be a curse upon anything. For the *throne* of God and the Lamb will be there, and *his* servants will worship *him*" (emphases added). If God and Jesus were two separate beings, wouldn't it have said *their* servants will worship *them*? Verse 4 says, "And they will see his face, and his name will be written on their foreheads." It mentions two— "God and the Lamb" and says they are one by saying, "his servants will worship him." It separates the two statements with a comma, meaning that they are still on the same subject.

**"Jesus and the Disciples Going to Emmaus"** by Gustave Doré

Luk 24:26-27 Ought not Christ to have suffered these things, and to enter into his glory? And beginning at Moses and all the prophets, he expounded unto them in all the scriptures the things concerning himself.

To see again that the Bible writers knew proper wording, go to Revelation 20:4 where it says, "Then I saw thrones, and the people sitting on them had been given authority to judge." Thrones, people, and them, all plural forms used in proper context, but when speaking of the throne of God and the Lamb it calls it one throne.

The last one we can see in Matthew 28:19 where it says to be baptized in the name (singular), of the Father, Son, and the Holy Ghost. That is three names given one singular name. That is the Trinity. One God, not three like some want to say, but one. If the ancient scribe wanted you to think they were three, he would have written baptized in the *names*, a plural form.

Look in 1 Samuel 17:13 in the King James Version, and we can see that it says, "and the names of his three eldest sons… were Eliab the first born, and next unto him Abinadab, and the third Shammah." Do you see here that when three separate persons are being named that the plural form, *names*, is used? No typo. It's in all translations I have seen. So, scripture names Father, Son, and Holy Ghost and gives it a singular "name." Then when naming three separate people, it uses the plural "names."

# Jesus Wants
# Thomas to Believe

*L*et's take a journey to John 20:24–31 and read what's there. Jesus has died on the cross and has not yet ascended to heaven. He appears to the disciples, and in verse 27 He tells Thomas, "Don't be faithless any longer. Believe!" He wants Thomas to believe something that he is not yet believing. At this point in Jesus's teaching, Thomas is still confused as to whom Jesus really is. He's just not getting the point. But Jesus is not confused. Jesus knows exactly who He is and what He is saying to and hearing from the disciples. To the disciples, Jesus has been their great teacher, their mentor, up to this point. Jesus knows exactly what He is doing and saying to the disciples. He now wants Thomas to believe something. He is trying to get him to understand an extremely vital point. What is it that Jesus wants Thomas to believe? What is it that Thomas just isn't getting? You don't have to wonder any more. Scripture lets us in on the mystery. Thomas, after touching Jesus's nail-scarred hands and placing his hand in the wound in Jesus's side from the spear, exclaims to Jesus in verse 28, "My Lord and my God!" So, Thomas in his excitement realizes at that very instant that Jesus is much more than he realized. He is not just a man but is, in fact, God in the flesh. Thomas calls out with great excitement. He is overjoyed at this new revelation and cries out, "My Lord and my God!" Some say that Thomas was still confused. That's just not what or even how it's written. It is written in a way that Thomas is calling Jesus Lord and God.

Jesus's very reply to Thomas calling him God was in verse 29 where He says to Thomas, "You believe because you have seen me. Blessed are those who believe without seeing me." Jesus wanted Thomas to believe just what He said: that He is our "Lord" and our "God." Because when Thomas called Jesus God, Jesus did not bat an eye but replied, you finally believe. Jesus sends out a special blessing to all those present, and those in the future, who believe that He is GOD without seeing Him right there in front of them because He says that very thing, more blessed is the one that believes without seeing.

Jesus is getting ready to send only these twelve men into the world to make disciples of the people. Don't you think that Jesus would have made sure that they knew everything correctly before He left them? If Jesus were not "my Lord and my God" as Thomas declared, I'm sure that He would have told him something different than what He did. Just what did He say when He was called God? Do you recollect? You finally believe, that is what was said. He wanted Thomas to believe that He himself, Jesus, is our Lord and our God. Thomas called Jesus God, and He did not refute the statement. Can I put it any other way? Jesus is God.

These three verses—27, 28, and 29—are very revealing information as to who Jesus is and who He wants the disciples to understand He is. Jesus was there teaching them the very Word of God. He gave them information that was not hidden, trickery, or vague. If anyone got what He was saying wrong, He ensured they had it correct. Thomas called Jesus God, and Jesus replied to him that you finally believe.

> "So pay attention to how you hear. To those who listen to my teaching, more understanding will be given. But to those who are not listening, even what they think they understand will be taken away from them." (Luke 8:18)

# A Title of Jesus

Jesus has many titles throughout scripture. We will focus on what I consider to be His most important title—God Almighty.

John 20:31 says, "But these are written so that you may continue to believe that Jesus is the Messiah, the Son of God..." What does it mean to be the "Son of God"? Is He a flesh and blood offspring of God like a human man and woman would have a child? Luke 1:32 says that Jesus "will be called the Son of the Most High"—a title. That means the "Son of God" is a title. A lot of people get confused about the title Son of God because they try to look at it in the same way we look at a father and son relationship between humans here on earth with our meager human understanding. It's not the same. With us, a father and a son are two separate people. Flesh and blood—one from the other. In the case of God, it's two separate ways in which God has made Himself known to us. One is God the Almighty being. The spirit form of God. The other is in the flesh as God the Son come to us in the form of a man—Jesus the Christ. Both existing as the same being—God.

In Isaiah 9:6 are more titles of the Messiah. This verse is a prophesy given to us about the coming Messiah. We see in the verse the titles of Wonderful Counselor, Mighty God, Everlasting Father, and Prince of Peace.

There is the title the Wonderful Counselor. That is the Holy Spirit—the Spirit that is in all of us telling us the right things to do and leading us in the Word of God.

Then we see the title Mighty God. Who but God is called mighty God? Is there any other God? No! I say not. Isaiah 43:10

says, "I alone am God. There is no other God—there never has been, and there never will be." God created many things and beings, but He did not create other gods. It just did not happen as some say.

We have Everlasting Father. The Messiah, who we know is Jesus from all the prophecies, is called our Everlasting Father. In Matthew 23:9 it says, "And don't address anyone here on earth as 'Father,' for only God in heaven is your spiritual Father." So, if the Messiah is Jesus and we can only address God as Father, then Jesus must be God. Romans 8:15 says we can now call God our Father. The verse reads, "So you have not received a spirit that makes you fearful slaves. Instead, you received God's Spirit when he adopted you as his own children. Now we call him, 'Abba, Father.'"

Prince of peace—the Son of God. Right there we have the Messiah (Jesus) called the Father, the Son, and the Holy Ghost, and that is what we call the Trinity—not three gods but one God in three distinct persons. Three ways in which we can know God.

Jesus has many titles ascribed to Him. But the title of Mighty God is by far His most important.

## THE EXACT IMAGE OF GOD

Go to John 10:22–38 and read where in verse 30 Jesus says, "the Father and I are one." Would you say that Jesus is saying that they are equal? One means one, the same one, and no other one doesn't it? Second Corinthians 4:4 says Jesus "is the exact likeness or image of God." An image reflects the original in equal manner does it not? Many other verses in scripture say that Jesus has all the "equal" characteristics of God. All that is God is attributed to Jesus. In Isaiah 40:25, God says, "to whom will you compare me? Who is my equal?" Scripture tells us that God has no equal, but Jesus is continually taking on the equal characteristics of God, putting Himself in the place of God, and taking credit for the things the Old Testament has credited to God Almighty alone. Philippians 2:6-8 says, "Though he was God, he did not think of equality with God as something to cling to. Instead, he gave up his divine privileges; he took the humble position of a slave and was born as a human being. When he appeared in human form, he humbled himself in obedience to God and died a criminal's death on a cross." Did Jesus think it not wrong to be equal to God? He is either blaspheming God, or Jesus is truly God Himself come to us in the flesh. What other man in all history could get away with taking on all the characteristics of God, and God not make him pay for it with his soul? Jesus is either God Himself or He is a crazy man that none of us should believe. I like to believe the former.

First Timothy 3:16 (KJV) says, "And without controversy great is the mystery of godliness: God was manifest in the flesh…" If you look at the definition of manifest, it means: to make clear or evident, reveal, *show itself*. Hmmm, then with that understanding in mind, we can say that Jesus is the bodily form of God the spirit. The Spirit God in the form of a man, Jesus. There it is, "Jesus, being in the form of God." It's right there in scripture. I'm not making this stuff up. Does God ever allow anyone to step into His shoes and assume the identity or role of God? No! He does not. Satan tried to put himself into the place of God and look where he is headed. (To hell and damnation, for those of you wondering.) Colossians 2:9 says, "For in him dwelleth all the fulness of the Godhead bodily." The Godhead? That is the Father, Son, and Holy Ghost—bodily.

Jesus is the exact likeness of God because He is God. He is the bodily form or manifestation of God the Spirit that we can see. In scripture it plainly says that Jesus was in the form of God. Remember in Genesis where it said, "Let us make man in our image." Jesus is that image spoken of. It just doesn't get any plainer than that. Jesus is God.

# THE JEWISH RELIGIOUS LEADERS

We are still in John 10. Look at verses 32 and 33. The religious leaders knew that Jesus was calling Himself God because they wanted to stone Him for blasphemy. Blasphemy is putting yourself in the place of God. They said to Him, "We're stoning you not for any good work, but for blasphemy! You, a mere man, claim to be God." They believed that Jesus was just a man. They did not see Him as the Messiah as the disciples did, let alone God himself. The Jewish leaders clearly understood what Jesus was saying when He claimed the title of the Son of God, and Jesus did not have to correct them as He always did to others. Jesus is referred to as the Teacher in John 1:49.

Verse 34 says, "I say, you are gods!" And that's how Jehovah's Witnesses justify saying that Jesus is just, "a god" rather than "the" God. In their Bible, the New World Translation, they changed the scripture in John 1:1 to say, "the word was a god" with a little "g" when clearly scripture says, "and the Word was God." But the next verse (35) clearly states that those who have been called "gods" are people receiving God's word *from* Jesus. Here it is in verses 35 and 36: "So if those people who received God's message were called 'gods,' why do you call it blasphemy when I say, 'I am the Son of God'? After all, the Father set me apart and sent me into the world." I know, you're saying, Look, He was sent by the Father! They are two! No! Not true. Look in Zechariah 2:10–11 and pay close attention to who is speaking. It reads:

"The LORD says, 'Shout and rejoice, O beautiful Jerusalem, for I am coming to live among you.

Many nations will join themselves to the LORD
on that day, and they, too, will be my people. I will
live among you, and you will know then the LORD
of the Heaven's Armies sent me to you.'"

Do you see it? It starts out with, "The LORD says." God is the one speaking. We know that when you see the word *LORD* in all capital letters in the Old Testament that it is referencing YAHWEH, and we know that YAHWEH is Almighty God— Jehovah. So, YAHWEH says, "I am coming to live among you, and you will know that Almighty Yahweh sent me to you." Who is *me* there? The *me* there is Yahweh. Don't you see it? God Almighty sent God to us. It does not say another God. It says God was sent to us. The Almighty spirit God, whom we can't see, came to us bodily by sending us Himself in the form of Jesus, who we can see. In Isaiah 45:18 we can see that the term *LORD* is God—Yahweh.

The Jewish religious leaders knew that Jesus calling Himself the Son of God was literally calling Himself God. In their times, you did not get stoned for blasphemy unless you were putting yourself in the place of God. Jesus asked them why they were so mad and wanted to stone Him. They said because He was making Himself God. If Jesus were not God, then why would He let the charade go on so long that it ended up with His brutal whipping and death on the cross? It's because He knew the truth that He was

21

God and the Jewish religious leaders denied that fact, and that's why they wanted to stone Him.

Another example is in Exodus 3:14–15 where God tells Moses to tell the Egyptians that His Eternal Holy name is "I AM." In John 8:58 when Jesus is again being questioned by the Jewish religious leaders, He quotes that passage in Exodus where God says His name is "I AM." Again, they wanted to stone Him for blasphemy.

**"Christ in the Synagogue"** by Gustave Doré

Mat 13:54 ...he taught them in their synagogue, insomuch that they were astonished, and said, Whence hath this *man* this wisdom, and *these* mighty works?

# When You Get to Heaven

Hebrews 1:10 says that the heavens are the work of Jesus's hand. Yet in Isaiah 44:24 God says, "By myself I made the earth and everything in it." Isaiah 45:12 says, "This is what the LORD says—your Redeemer and Creator: 'I am the LORD, who made all things. I alone stretched out the heavens. Who was with me when I made the earth?'" That is God saying that He made the earth alone, by himself. He said, "who was with me." Yet once again, in Hebrews 1:10 it states that Jesus's hands made the heavens. I would be really confused if I didn't know the fact that the two—Jesus and God—are one and the same being. The Word of God is what the Bible is, and it says that Jesus is God many times in scripture. So, there is no problem when it jumps back and forth using both names in the same instances. Not to the learned reader. There's unison in the Bible when you recognize Jesus as being God.

Do you see how the Bible writers interchange between God and Jesus with the same attributes? They ascribe the same things and instances to the two as if they were one. That's because the entire Bible from start to finish, which was written by forty-plus authors over a fifteen-hundred-year period in sixty-six different books, is talking about the same being—God. They knew it.

Zechariah 14:9 says that "there will be one Lord", in the Old

Testament, where we have seen that all capital letters in *LORD* means God. There will be only one God in heaven.

Revelation 21:1–8 says that "God Himself" will live with us. Here we know that Jesus is the one talking because it states, "I am the Alpha and the Omega—the Beginning and the End." It then goes on to say that He (Jesus) will be our God when He is physically living with humankind.

Revelation 22:13 says that Jesus is the "First and the Last." To connect this phrase with God and Jesus, we see that Isaiah 41:4 says, "It is I, the LORD, the First and the Last. I alone am he." God says that He *alone* is God, but in Revelation we see Jesus being giving the same title of the "First and the Last." Both Jesus and God can only be the First and the Last because they are the same being.

When you get to heaven, if you do—and it's entirely your choice—you will not see Jesus and God. You will only see Jesus, who is God!

## Jesus Is the Holy Spirit

Let's look at another scripture given to us in the book of John. In John 14:1–31, the disciples want to see the Father. Jesus has nearly completed His teachings to the disciples. He tells them in verse 6 that "I am the way, the truth, and the life. *No one* can come to the Father except through me" (emphasis mine). Yet Ephesians 2:18 states, "Now all of us can come to the Father through the same Holy Spirit because of what Christ has done for us." The gospels and the letters teach us that Jesus is the only way we can come to the Father. We see in Acts 4:12 that it says, "There is Salvation in no one else! God has given no other name under heaven by which we must be saved." Jesus even told them that He is the only way to the Father. We must then conclude that the "Holy Spirit" spoken of in Ephesians 2:18 is Christ Himself.

We know that the Holy Spirit is God and now we see that Jesus is that Holy Spirit. So that means Jesus is God or the Bible is just a garbled mess of worthless ancient sayings that make no sense at all. First Corinthians 14:33 says, "For God is not a God of disorder but of peace..." If you read the scriptures as the Father, Son, and Holy Ghost being three separate entities, then it is confusing and makes no true sense at all because they are all contained in the same topics and instances ascribed to one being. Therefore, we must conclude that Jesus is the Holy Spirit.

Moving on, 2 Corinthians 3:14–18 shows us again that Jesus and the Holy Spirit are the same being. Verse 14 says, "But the people's minds were hardened, and to this day whenever the old covenant is being read, the same veil covers their minds so they cannot understand the truth. And this veil can be removed only by believing In Christ." Verse 16 reads, "But whenever someone turns to the Lord, the veil is taken away." In these two verses, we see the veil is only removed by the Lord: Christ. Scripture just connected these two terms for Jesus: Lord and Christ. Now verse 17 connects the Lord (Jesus) with the Spirit (Holy Ghost): "For the Lord is the Spirit, and wherever the Spirit of the Lord is, there is freedom." The Spirit is also linked to "the Spirit of the Lord." So, we have Jesus being given the title of the Spirit.

Galatians 4:6 says, "God has sent the Spirit of his Son into your hearts, prompting us to call out, 'Abba, Father.'" We only have one true Father, and Isaiah lets us know that is the Messiah. Isaiah 9:6 says, "Everlasting Father," one of Christ's titles. I know you're saying that Galatians 4:6 is saying God sent His son. You need to remember the verses we have previously read in Zechariah 2:10–11 where Yahweh Almighty (God) sent Yahweh (Jesus).

> "This Salvation was something even the prophets wanted to know more about when they prophesied about this gracious salvation prepared for you. They wondered what time or situation the Spirit of Christ within them was talking about when he told them in advance about Christ's suffering and his great glory afterward. They were told that their messages were not for themselves, but for you. And now this

Good News has been announced to you by those who preached in the power of the Holy Spirit sent from heaven. It is all so wonderful that even the angels are eagerly watching these things happen." (1 Peter 1:10–12)

Do you see the connections here between Christ and the Holy Spirit? It's there. A similar phrase was used by Zechariah. It says that the spirit of Christ prophesied about the suffering of Christ to the prophets of the Old Testament. Christ existed before He was born a man. First Corinthians 2:12 says that "we have received God's spirit." You will see later where scripture says that there is only one Spirit.

Romans 8:9 connects the Spirit of God with the Spirit of Christ. It reads, "You are controlled by the Spirit if you have the Spirit of God living in you. (And remember that those who do not have the Spirit of Christ living in them do not belong to him at all.)" First the verse starts out calling the Spirit the Spirit of God, then it calls the same Spirit the Spirit of Christ. It connects Spirit, Spirit of God, and Spirit of Christ. That is the Holy Spirit, the Father, and the Son, respectively. That is what we call the Trinity right there. God tells us in 1 Corinthians 2:5 that we need to "trust not in human wisdom but in the power of God."

In 1 Corinthians 2:10–16 we are told that God has given us

His Spirit and that the disciples speak words given to them by the Spirit, using the Spirit's words to explain spiritual truths. We know the disciples received their words through Jesus, the Word of God. Is this making any sense to you yet? Jesus is the Holy Spirit through whom they received their words. John 14:26 says, "But when the Father sends the Advocate as my representative—that is, the Holy Spirit—he will teach you everything and well remind you of everything I have told you." Now we know that the Holy Spirit is God's Spirit, and it says that the Holy Spirit is Jesus's representative? Whoa! If Jesus was not God, then this would not make any sense. God would never be representative of man. If Jesus were just a man. We can only come in God's name, not God in man's name. Jesus is not just a man; He is God in the flesh. We already saw that in 1 Timothy 3:16 (KJV), where it stated, "God was manifest in the flesh."

In 1 Corinthians 1:24 we see "Christ is the power of God and the wisdom of God." Ephesians 3:20 says, "Now glory be to God, who is able, through his mighty power at work within us, to accomplish infinitely more than we might ask or think." Romans 15:19 says, "They were convinced by the power of miraculous signs and wonders and by the power of God's Spirit..." In 2 Corinthians 12:9 it says, "... the power of Christ may rest upon me." It does not say the power of God working through me. It says, "power of Christ." I thought it was the power of God. The Bible writers were not slipping when they wrote such phrases. They were being led by the Holy Spirit, and they knew that what they were being led to write was true. The two are one. They knew this to be true, so it was not a problem for them to interchange the names with one another. (i.e., God, Jesus, Christ, Holy Spirit, Lord, etc.)

First Corinthians 2:14 is an eye-opener. It says people who aren't Christians can't understand these truths from God's Spirit. The next verse puts it all in perspective. It states that God gave us His Spirit and then says in verse 16, "But we understand these things, for we have the mind of Christ." So, scripture connects God's Spirit, who we know is the Holy Spirit, with Jesus.

First Corinthians 3:16 says, "the Spirit of God lives in you." We know that there is only one Spirit, so Christ is the Spirit of God living in me. Galatians 2:20 says, "Christ lives in me." If he were merely a man, He could not live in me. See 2 Corinthians 5:16 where it says, "At one time we thought of Christ merely from a human point of view. How differently we know him now!" And they say it with excitement! They once thought of Jesus as just a man.

Isaiah 63:7–14 says the "Spirit of the Lord" was there when the Israelites wandered through the desert for forty years. That was Jesus! First Corinthians 10:1–5 says that Jesus was with the Israelites wandering in the desert. It says that they "drank from the spiritual rock that traveled with them, and that rock was Christ."

They wandered in the desert around one thousand years before Jesus was born a man. We can say that the Spirit, the Holy Spirit, the Spirit of God, the Spirit of Christ, and the Spirit of the Lord, let's not forget God's Spirit, are all one Spirit by what Ephesians 4:4–6 says: "There is one body and one Spirit…, one Lord, one faith…, one God and father."

Look what 1 John 3:2 says: "We will see him as he really is" speaking of Jesus. Throughout biblical history, we have known God in many ways as God Almighty, the Holy Spirit, and in His human form as Jesus. A similar passage in Zechariah 14:9 states: "And the Lord will be King over all the earth. On that day there be one LORD—his name alone will be worshipped." That's an extremely revealing verse about our Lord: His name will be one. Need I say more? Christ cannot be my Lord and my God if He is not the one God (Deuteronomy 6:4).

**"The Last Judgment"** *by Gustave Doré*

Rev 20:12 And I saw the dead, small and great, stand before God; and the books were opened: and another book was opened, which is *the book* of life: and the dead were judged out of those things which were written ....

# Jesus Raised Himself from the Dead

C hrist is the part of God that we can see. The only thing we will ever see—His image (Colossians 1:15). In John 10:18 Jesus says, "No one can take my life from me. I sacrifice it voluntarily. For I have the authority to lay it down when I want to and also to take it up again…" In John 2:19 Jesus says to the Jewish leaders that are looking for a sign: "Destroy this temple, and in three days I will raise it up." He says, "I" will raise it up. Not that God or some other power would. If He is not God, then He was just a dead man on the cross. How would, or could, He raise himself from the dead? How does He have the power to raise Himself from the dead? Romans 10:9 says, "If you openly declare that Jesus is Lord and believe in your heart that God raised him from the dead, you will be saved." That fact—that God raised Him from the dead—is one of the main facts God wants you to believe for your salvation. So, we need to know who really raised Him from the dead.

In one verse we have Jesus saying He will raise Himself and in another verse we have it saying God raised Him from the dead. Do you see how the Bible writers interchanged God and Jesus in different verses? They knew that God and Jesus were the same being. The Bible seems contradictory if you read it with the thought that Jesus and God are separate beings. But when you read it with the knowledge that Jesus and God are one and the same being, as the disciples finally realized, then verses like these make sense. These are not typographical errors in scripture. They are fact! They are there for the mature Christian to seek out and find.

Luke 11:9 says, "And so I tell you, keep on asking, and you will receive what you ask for. Keep on seeking, and you will find. Keep on knocking, and the door will be opened to you." God will give you understanding of the Bible if you ask Him for it. Don't rely on anyone else to tell you what scripture means. Not even this book I've written. I'm just a man. Put your faith in the Holy Spirit and search it out for yourself. God will not mislead you as so many other so-called godly men are doing today and have been doing since the days of the disciples.

"If you look for me wholeheartedly, you will find me." (Jeremiah 29:13)

In John 5:39 Jesus says the "Scriptures" point to Him. "Scriptures" is plural. He said all scripture points to Him, and we know that God is not the author of confusion (1 Corinthians 14:33). Jesus will raise Himself from the dead because He is the mighty power and wisdom of God (1 Corinthians 1:24). Jesus, as God, raised Himself from the dead after being crucified on the cross. Jesus can raise Himself because He never died in Spirit. He only died as Jesus in human form but always remained God in Spirit form. Your body will die, but your spirit will immediately be with God. Scripture says to be absent from the body is to be present with the Lord in 2 Corinthians 5:8.

In conclusion, to answer the question of who raised Jesus from the dead, we have to say that Jesus raised Himself from the dead because He is God, and God can never die. Once the body of Jesus closed His eyes and His heart stopped beating, He was once again back in the Spirit form of God Almighty. Our bodies will die and return to the dust, but our spirits will live on as God's Spirit did from the cross.

# GOD'S ATTRIBUTES ASCRIBED TO JESUS

Let's see what attributes of God we could ascribe to Jesus:

God's power and wisdom    1 Corinthians 1:24
God's spirit             2 Corinthians 3:14–18
God's Word               John 1:1

| | |
|---|---|
| God's equality | John 5:16–24 |
| God's glory | 2 Corinthians 4:6 |
| God's blood | Acts 20:28 |
| God's fullness | Colossians 1:19, 2:9 |
| God's name Immanuel means | Matthew 1:23 |
| "God with us" | |
| The creator | John 1:3, Colossians 1:15–17 |
| God's love | Entire Bible |
| His Omnipotence | 2 Thessalonians 2:9, Hebrews 1:3 |
| His Omnipresence | Ephesians 1:23 |
| His Omniscience | Colossians 2:3, John 16:30 |
| God's image | Colossians 1:15, Hebrews 1:3 |

Could you be all those attributes of something and not be that exact same being? I say not! And scripture agrees. We have already read that God tells us that no one is His equal. These are only a few of the attributions out of scripture. There are so many, many more.

# WILL I SEE GOD?

The disciples wanted to see God. I would like to see God and one day I along with everyone who ever lived will. Who wouldn't want to see God—our maker? In 1 Timothy 6:16 we read: "No human eye has ever seen him, nor ever will." Nor ever will? Then, who will we see in Revelation 21:3 where it states: "Look, God's home is now among his people! He will live with them, and they will be his people. God himself will be with them." Have we found a contradiction in scripture? We see also in Zechariah 8:3 that it says, "And now the Lord says: I am returning to Mount Zion, and I will live in Jerusalem." Isaiah 30:20 says, "Though the Lord gave you adversity for food and suffering for drink, he will still be with you to teach you. You will see your teacher with your own eyes." You will see Christ as He truly is—God! That's found in 1 John 3:2.

God Himself will be there for your eyes to behold. What will that be? We will see God's glory; His image—Jesus. Jesus is the one who said if you believe, then you will "see God's glory" in John 11:40. Scripture tells us what that is and where you can find it in 2 Corinthians 4:6, where it says, "For God, who said, 'Let there be light in the darkness,' has made this light shine in our hearts so we could know the glory of God that is seen in the face of Jesus Christ." That means we can say that Jesus's glory is God's glory.

Turn now to Habakkuk 2:14. It says there that, "For as the waters fill the sea, the earth will be filled with an awareness of the glory of the LORD." And right there in 2 Corinthians 3:18 it says, "So all of us who have had that veil removed can see and reflect the glory of the Lord. And the Lord—who is the Spirit—makes us more and more like him as we are changed into his glorious image."

37

We just determined that the glory of God is seen in the face of Christ Jesus. That indicates Jesus is God's glory. Yet in Isaiah 42:8 it reads: "I am the LORD; that is my name! I will not give my glory to anyone else, nor share my praise with carved idols." God puts it out there that He will not share His glory. He's adamant about it. If they are not the same being, then God just lied, and we know that God can't lie (Titus 1:2). All the emphasis on the glory of Jesus would take away from God's glory, *if* they were two separate beings. Fortunately, they are not.

After seeing God say He gives His glory to no one, we read in John 17:5 Jesus saying, "Now, Father, bring me into the glory we shared before the world began." *They cannot share the glory*! God specifically says He does not share His glory with anyone. This is an extraordinarily strong indication that they are one and the same being. When you read the Bible with the knowledge that Jesus is God, then each of these passages that interchange God, Jesus, and the Holy Spirit make perfect sense. But conversely, when you read the Bible thinking that Jesus and God are two separate beings, then the Bible seems to be full of contradictions, false statements, and outright lies not to be believed.

First John 1:18 says, "No one has ever seen God. But the unique One, who is himself God, is near to the Father's heart. He has revealed God to us." But we see that Moses said that he sat with God face to face as one sits with a friend. Here it is in Exodus 33:11:

"Inside the Tent of Meeting, the LORD would speak to Moses face to face, as one speaks to a friend." Who and what was Moses seeing?

First Timothy 6:16 says that, "He alone can never die, and he lives in light so brilliant that no human can approach him. No human eye has ever seen him, nor ever will. All honor and power to him forever! Amen."

You can find where Jacob wrestled with God physically in Genesis 32:1–32. He was astonished of the mere fact that he would die because he saw "God face to face" but lived to tell about it. I thought we just read in 1 Timothy that no one has ever seen God or ever will?

> "Christ is the visible image of the invisible God. He existed before anything was created and is supreme over all creation..." (Colossians 1:15)

Will anyone ever see God? Will our eyes ever behold the glory of our maker? Is the Bible contradicting itself? This back and forth is so confusing. No, the Bible is not contradicting itself, and it is truthful in what it says, and yes, of course you will see God! Scripture says that you will. You don't have to fret anymore. You will see God! He will be in the form of a man—Jesus in all His glory is what you will see. God's Spirit lives in the physical human body of Jesus. Colossians 1:19 says, "For God in all his fullness was pleased to live in Christ..." God in the form of a man is what you will see, and that man is Jesus. Crisis averted.

## "Jacob Wrestling with the Angel" by Gustave Doré

Gen 32:24 ...and there wrestled a man with him until the breaking of the day. ...he touched the hollow of his thigh; and the hollow of Jacob's thigh was out of joint, as he wrestled with him.

# JESUS CLAIMS TO BE THE FATHER

Let's explore what Jesus says in John 14:1. Here in Christ's own words He claims to be the Father. He says, "Don't let your hearts be troubled. Trust in God, and trust also in me." Up to this point in Jesus's ministry He has been a great teacher to the disciples. But now He is nearing the end of His time on earth and going back to heaven soon. He gives the disciples some information that He had not yet given them. Up until now they have known Him as, "the Son of God."

Look at Hebrews 5:11–6:3. Christ now wants to give them some further information past the first principles of the oracles of God. He wants to move past the basics of Christianity and into a more mature understanding of the Word of God. If Jesus had just come out when He first began teaching and blurted out to the masses that He was God, how many people do you think would have given Him the time of day? Not many, I presume. They would have just looked at Him as another lunatic out there in the world claiming divinity. Enough didn't listen to Him even coming as the Son of God with all the miracles He performed. Would you listen to someone today that came out and said, "Hey, look at me, I'm God"? Probably not. Well, you shouldn't. Jesus warns us of many to come claiming to be him. In Matthew 24:4-5 it says, "Don't let anyone mislead you, for many will come in my name, claiming, 'I am the Messiah.' They will deceive many." Don't you be deceived.

The disciples are still confused as to what Jesus is trying to say. In John 14:7, Jesus is quoted as saying, "If you had really known me, you would know who my Father is." Then He goes on to tell them an extremely revealing statement. He said, "From now on, you know him, and have seen him!" He says it with excitement! He has not yet come out and blatantly said that He is God the Father. We have already seen in Ephesians 4:5 that there is only "one God and Father." But now He feels they are mature enough in their understanding to even fathom the notion that He is God.

Who are the disciples looking at when Jesus, speaking of God said, "You have seen Him"? They were looking at Jesus! But Jesus being in human form, they were still confused, and in John 4:8 Phillip replies, "Lord, show us the Father, and we will be satisfied." They want to see God, and Jesus replies in verse 9, "Have I been with you all this time, Philip, and yet you still don't know who I am? Anyone who has seen me has seen the Father! So why are you asking me to show him to you?" He says in verse 10, "Don't you believe that I am in the Father and the Father is in me?" They seemed to be confused as to who Jesus really was just as people today are.

The disciples want to see God the Father. Jesus goes straight to the point, telling them, I am God. He said you see God. I'm right here in front of you. Jesus is God standing right there in front of them and they remain in a state of confusion. They still did not grasp the fact that He was God in the flesh. They stayed confused until Jesus died on the cross and returned to them, and Thomas placed his hand in Jesus's wounds. That's when they finally realized, as we saw Thomas put it, the fact that Jesus is our Lord and our God.

# Jesus, the Voice of the Holy Spirit in Us

*J*esus came to earth as our example to imitate (1 Thessalonians 1:6). He's telling us to listen to that voice inside of us that will lead us to the truth and right living. I know that people say Jesus talks to God, so they must be two. No! That's not the case at all. Jesus said He would live in us. He is that voice inside of us—the Holy Spirit—urging us to do right.

> "This is the new covenant I will make with my people on
> that day, says the LORD: I will put my laws in their hearts,
> and I will write them on their minds." (Hebrews 10:16)

Jesus wants us to imitate Him. He says to be holy because He is holy in 1 Peter 1:16. Listen to that voice inside when it's telling you the right things to do. Do you sometimes talk to yourself and your conscience talk to you? Sometimes you talk out loud to yourself, but are you one being or two?

God says, "… I will guide you along the best pathway for your life. I will advise you and watch over you." (Psalms 32:8) Look at it this way. You know that little voice in your head that tells you right from wrong, the voice that's always challenging your daily decisions? Do you control it? No, you do not. I don't control mine, but it's always telling me the right things to do. I sometimes go against it, and it always gets me in trouble. My carnal mind usually overrides what my conscience determines and is telling me is the right thing to do.

Once I've chosen to go against it, I end up saying something to the effect of, "I knew I should have done this or that" or, "I told myself not to do that." Hmmm, I told myself not to do something. That sounds a lot like Jesus saying that He only does what the Father tells Him to do. Jesus is trying to get us to realize that that voice inside us is God.

Remember that Jesus is our example to follow (1 Peter 2:21). He came here to show us how to get to Him. He wanted us to follow Him. If we were to listen to that voice inside our hearts and only follow what it tells us is the right thing to do, then we would be much holier people and much better off. That voice is Christ living in us and directing us (Galatians 4:6, 5:16–26; 1 John 4:7–5:21). That voice we call a conscience is the Spirit of God; the Holy Spirit, or you can call it the Spirit of Christ. It's all the same thing. He is living in us and leading us to the truth (Romans 8:5–9).

Now on the other hand, if your conscious is leading you to do evil things, then you are being led by Satan, and you can only rid yourself of him through turning to Christ. You should let Christ into your heart—invite Him in. He is there knocking at your door, but you must invite Him in (Revelation 3:20). Christ forces Himself on no one. He leaves that choice up to each one of use. You either want Him in your life or you do not. Don't deny His gracious gift of salvation (Ephesians 2:8). Invite Him in today.

> "I don't really understand myself, for I want to do
> what is right, but I don't do it. Instead, I do what I
> hate." (Romans 7:15)

Satan can mislead you in your heart. Second Corinthians 11:14 says, "Even Satan can disguise himself as an angel of light." He is out there deceiving you into thinking that God is not real. If Satan is real, that is a good indication that God must be real, for He created Satan. Read Ephesians 2:1–10. Satan is a spirit that pulls you away from God. That is the evil conscience in this world. He is "the commander of the powers in the unseen world. He is the spirit at work in the hearts of those who refuse to obey God." We also see that "Satan, who is the god of this world, has blinded the minds of those who don't believe. They are unable to see the glorious light of the Good News. They don't understand this message about the glory of Christ, who is the exact likeness of God." (2 Corinthians 4:4) If you continue following this evil spirit in you, you will share in his fate, which is the "lake of fire" (Revelation 19:20, 20:11–15, 21:8). Verse 8 in Revelation 21 tells of those who do not go against that evil nature (conscience). Their fate is not one you should follow.

Jesus, as the Holy Spirit in all of us, can be there directing you to right living. All you must do is to invite Him into your heart. He gives you the choice. He did not create us as non-thinking robots. God gave us the ability to make our own decisions in life. We are free. You either want God with His teachings and the gift of salvation, or you don't. It's once again up to you. Accept this gift today.

# YOUR SPIRIT—YOU

Let's look at your spirit now. Yes, you are a spirit. You know that "Christ is the visible image of the invisible God." (Colossians 1:15) Christ is all we will ever see of God's spirit. Your body is what we see of your spirit. We are all made in the image of God. But Christ is "*the* exact likeness of God." (2 Corinthians 4:4) He is *the* image of God. We are made *in* His image. That's why we all look different and are not clones. Jesus is the exact image of God. We are made in the image, similar, but not exact.

Can your body live without your spirit? No, it cannot. Look in Job 34:14–15. It says, "If God were to take back His Spirit and withdraw His breath, all life would cease, and humanity would turn again to dust." But your spirit can live without your body. We are all just spirits, and God gave us bodies just as He gave Himself one, in the form of Jesus. Second Corinthians 5:1–10 says, "we will not be spirits without bodies." While we live in these bodies (earthly), we are not at home with the Lord. Romans 8:10 states: "And Christ lives within you, so even though your body will die because of sin, the Spirit gives you life because you have been made right with God." My point is that Christ Jesus is the body that God lives in. Your body is where your spirit dwells. We have already seen in Colossians 1:19 that it says, "For God in all his fullness was pleased to live in Christ..." "All His fullness," it says. Not some or part, but *all.* Your body is where your spirit lives, all of it. Part of God lives in me, but not all of Him, or the fullness. Colossians 2:9 goes a little deeper. It says, "For in Christ the Fullness of God lives in a human body." Is it any clearer than that? The Spirit of God lives in the body of the man Jesus just like your spirit lives in the body that is you. In 2 Corinthians 5:3 it says that "we will put on heavenly bodies; we will not be spirits without bodies."

The "you" that makes up you is your spirit, not the physical body that you can see with your eyes. One day these bodies that we live in will rot in the ground. But one day, God will give us new, spiritual bodies that will last forever. They will be physical and not ghosts, like Jesus said to the disciples in Luke 24:39 when He appeared to them after He was crucified but before He ascended to heaven. He said, "Look at my hands. Look at my feet. You can see that it's really me. Touch me and make sure that I am not a ghost, because ghosts don't have bodies, as you see that I do." Unlike our bodies today, these spiritual bodies will go on for eternity and not wear out.

Do you understand now what your body is? It is the vessel in which your spirit lives. This body will die and turn again to dust. But your spirit that is the real you will live on. Jesus is the body that the Spirit of God lives in. Jesus is God in the flesh as scripture tells us.

"The Sermon on the Mount" *by Gustave Doré*

Mat 5:7-10 Blessed *are* the merciful: for they shall obtain mercy. ...
Blessed *are* the peacemakers: for they shall be called the children of God.
Blessed *are* they which are persecuted for righteousness' sake: ....

# Jesus—the Holy Spirit

Let's look at Jesus's claims in John 14:15–18. He says that He will send the Advocate or Counselor, who we already learned is the Holy Spirit. That's also in one of the Messiah's names in Isaiah 9:6, as I've mentioned earlier. Pay close attention to verse 17. Jesus says that the world doesn't recognize the Holy Spirit but that the disciples do. Here is the important part: He goes on to say the Holy Spirit lives with you now and later will be in you. He had not yet given them the Holy Spirit (John 7:39, 14:26, 16:12–14; Acts 1:4–2:40). He didn't need to because He is the Holy Spirit, and He is with them in the flesh at the moment. The Holy Spirit in them would be there to guide them when He was physically not there with them anymore. We went over earlier where Jesus said that you see God when the disciples wanted to see the Father. Here He says that the Holy Spirit lives with them now.

Jesus is the Holy Spirit that's living with them now as we see He just stated. He said, "and later will be in you." While Jesus was standing there with them, there was no need for Him to be in them in the form of the Holy Spirit. He also says, "I will come to you." Do you see it? Why would He have to come to them? He was already there with them. He was talking of sending the Holy Spirit to them after His ascension, and He states, "I will come to you." He was not talking about His Second Coming, as we can plainly see that has not occurred yet. In Acts 1:4–5, Jesus tells them not to leave Jerusalem until they received what He promised them. He said that in a few days they would be "baptized with the Holy Spirit."

Jesus continues on in John 18 and says, "No, I will not abandon you as orphans—I will come to you." Do you see? Jesus is preparing to leave them physically. Jesus says in verse 16 that the Father would send the Advocate, but in John 16:7 Jesus says, "But in fact, it is best for you that I go away, because if I don't, the Advocate won't come. If I do go away, then I will send him to you." It plainly says the Father would send the Advocate, and then Jesus says He will be the one sending the Advocate. The Father is the "I" here and the "I" is Jesus. Are the Bible writers confused? Did the Bible get misinterpreted? Or is this just what God wanted them to write? Jesus will send the Advocate because He is God.

Go to John 16:12–14. It says that the Holy Spirit (Advocate) will bring Jesus glory by revealing what He receives from Jesus. We already know that God gives His glory to no one else (Isaiah 42:8). And if Jesus is not God, then how does the Holy Spirit, who we know is the Spirit of God Almighty in 1 Corinthians 2:12, reveal what He receives from Jesus? Did God get the Word from Jesus, or is Jesus the Word? Jesus also says that all the Father has is His. That would be awfully arrogant for someone to say if he were just a man. It's said in 2 Corinthians 5:16 that the disciples once thought of Jesus as just a man.

Jesus is the Holy Spirit spoken of here. He now lives in us and encourages us to do His will. Jesus left the earth over two thousand years ago and now lives in and communicates with us as the Holy Spirit inside of us. He vowed to return physically just as He left, in a cloud ascending to heaven but now lives in us spiritually until the day He returns. And I don't hesitate to say that in today's world with all the tensions between Christians and the Muslim world that it may be sooner than later. You can see the world dividing up into the true believers full of love and understanding and the other side of hate, violence, and deception.

Allow Jesus's Holy Spirit into your heart today before it's too late.

"The Apostles Preaching the Gospel" by Gustave Doré

Act 2:32-33 This Jesus hath God raised up, whereof we all are witnesses. ... and having received of the Father the promise of the Holy Ghost, he hath shed forth this, which ye now see and hear.

# THE MIGHTY KING

Now let's delve into the scriptures that reveal to us who the mighty King truly is. There can only be one true King. Turn to Isaiah 43:15. God says He is the creator of Israel and is their King. Isaiah 44:6 says God is the King of Israel. Yet in apparent contrast John 1:49 has Nathanael saying to Jesus, "Rabbi, you are the Son of God—the King of Israel." Then you go to Psalm 10:16, and you see where it says the LORD, meaning Yahweh, "is king forever and ever", and Psalms 29:10 says the "LORD reigns as king forever."

Psalm 95:3 says that "the LORD is a great God, a great King above all gods." So, if Jesus is "a god" as the Jehovah's Witnesses would have you believe, then how can He be "King"? We will soon see the truth in scripture.

Let's take an in-depth look at Isaiah 6:1–13 and compare it to Revelation 4:1–11. Isaiah says he saw the Lord sitting on a throne and His robe filled the temple. John in Revelation says he saw heaven standing open and a throne with someone sitting on it. They both describe mighty beings around it with six wings. The beings are singing the same song in each account: "Holy, holy, holy is the LORD of Heaven's Armies!" From this song and what each prophet described in each account, it's safe to say they were both seeing God on this throne. In verse 5 Isaiah says that he has seen "the King, the LORD of Heaven's Armies." In Revelation,

John connects this with Jesus by stating in Revelation 4:8, "the Lord God, the Almighty—the one who always was, who is, and is still to come." By that verse saying, "is still to come," we know that Jesus is the one that all creation is waiting to come. Even the Muslims are waiting for His return.

We can further connect verse 8 to Jesus by looking at Revelation 1:7. It says, "Look! He comes with the clouds of heaven. And everyone will see him—even those who pierced him…" Compare the "clouds of heaven" to Matthew 24:30. There it says, "And they will see the Son of Man coming on the clouds of heaven with power and great glory." The second part of Revelation 1:7 says, "And everyone will see him—even those who pierced him," which is a reference to God in Zechariah 12:10. It says, "They will look upon me whom they have pierced and mourn for him as for an only son. They will grieve bitterly for him as for a firstborn son who has died." The *me* is meaning they will be looking at God and the *him* is meaning they will mourn for Jesus. Was God ever pierced? It was Jesus on the cross who was pierced and who they looked upon. Isaiah, though, says God was the one being crucified and pierced.

Revelation 4:9–11 makes further connections to Jesus in key phrases that speak only of Him. Verse 9 states that the one on the throne is the, "one who lives forever and ever." This is a direct reference to Jesus in Revelation 1:18. It says, "I am the living one.

I died, but look—I am alive forever and ever! And I hold the keys of death and the grave."

Both prophets writing hundreds of years apart are writing of the same vision of seeing God. Isaiah in Old Testament times is seeing God on the throne, and John in New Testament times is seeing Jesus sitting on the throne as Almighty God. Jesus is the King. He is God Almighty. The Mighty King.

## KING OF KINGS, LORD OF LORDS

There are many references to "the King of kings, Lord of lords" in scripture. There can only be one with this title. You can't have two different people with the same title or it's just not believable. I will show you through scripture that this title is given to Jesus and to God.

In Revelation 17:14, the Lamb is "Lord of all lords and King of all kings." We see also in Revelation 19:16 the title "King of all kings, Lord of all lords" written on Christ's robe and His thigh. Those are both reverences to Jesus being King of kings.

In 1 Timothy 6:15–16 we read, "almighty God, the King of all kings and Lord of all lords." In Psalm 136:1–26, God is ascribed the title, "God of gods" and "Lord of lords." Deuteronomy 10:17 says, "For the LORD your God is the God of gods and Lord of lords. He is the great God, the mighty and awesome God, who shows no partiality and cannot be bribed."

Is there a mistake in the Word of God or is Jesus what is written: God of gods and Lord of lords? Both are ascribed the same titles. This is another fact in scripture showing that Jesus is God.

Isaiah 40:8 says, "The grass withers and flowers fade, but the word of our God stands forever." Must I say more?

## JESUS CONNECTED TO THE SPIRIT

In the book of Revelation, seven letters are written to the seven churches of Asia. All of them begin with the phrase "This is the message from the one who," except for the one from the angel to the church of Thyatira. It says from the Son of God. All of them are references to Jesus that can be cross-referenced in Revelation 1:8–19.

When you get to the end of each letter, you will see the same message: "Anyone with ears to hear must listen to the Spirit and understand what he is saying to the churches." We know by the opening two verses in Revelation 1 that Jesus's testimony is being recorded here. But it says, "understand the Spirit." Here, yet again, is another reference to Jesus being "the Spirit" and scripture trying to get the reader to "listen" and "understand."

Christ tells us in John 5:39: "You search the Scriptures because you believe they give you eternal life. But the Scriptures point to me!" Notice He says "Scriptures," as in all of them and says it with excitement. He does not specify any certain ones. He just uses the plural form of the word.

I'll go over each one, church by church, so you can see. Remember as you read that these are all references to Jesus given to John by the Spirit.

# Ephesus

"This is the message from the one who holds the seven stars in his right hand, the one who walks among the seven golden lampstands." (Revelation 2:1)

"And standing in the middle of the lampstands was someone like the Son of Man." (Revelation 1:13)

"The seven stars are angels of the seven churches." (Revelation 1:20)

The "Son of Man" is referring to Jesus in Mark 14:62 and many other places in the New Testament. We have this message here connecting Jesus and the Spirit by showing the Son of Man is in the middle of the lampstands as it says the Spirit is in Revelation 2:1.

# Smyrna

"This is the message from the one who is the First and the Last, who was dead but is now alive." (Revelation 2:8)

There are two parts to this verse. First, here are references to the First and the Last: In Revelation 1:17 Jesus says, "I am the First and the Last." In Revelation 22:13 He says, "I am the Alpha and Omega, the First and the Last, the beginning and the End."

The next verses refer to God. Isaiah 41:4 says, "It is I, the LORD, the First and the Last. I alone am he." Isaiah 44:6 says, "I am the First and the Last; there is no other God." Isaiah 48:12 states: "I alone am God, the First and the Last." Both Jesus and God can only be the First and the Last if, and only if, they are one. They can't be two separate beings or the Bible is one messed-up book.

The second part is Revelation 1:18: "I am the living one. I died, but look—I am alive for ever and ever!" The one who died is Jesus. Revelation 15:7 says, "...of God, who lives for ever and ever," referring to God. Revelation 10:6 says "in the name of the one who lives forever and ever" referring to the creator God.

# Pergamum

"This is the message from the one with the sharp two-edged sword." (Revelation 2:12)

Revelation 19:11–21 has it in verse 15 that from Jesus's mouth came a sharp sword. Revelation 1:16 says "and a sharp two-edged sword came from his mouth."

Ephesians 6:17 says "the sword of the Spirit, which is the word of God." The sword spoken of here is not a literal sword; it's speaking of the Word of God coming out of the mouth of Jesus. It will sting the minds of those opposed to His teachings.

# Thyatira

"This is the message from the Son of God, whose eyes are like flames of fire, whose feet are like polished bronze." (Revelation 2:18)

"And his eyes were like flames of fire. His feet were like polished bronze refined in a furnace." (Revelation 1:14–15)

"His eyes were like flames of fire … and his title was the Word of God." (Revelation 19:11–21) All descriptions here are given to both Jesus and the Spirit.

# Sardis

This is the message from the one who has the sevenfold Spirit of God and the seven stars." (Revelation 3:1)

"And in front of the throne were seven torches with burning flames. They are the sevenfold Spirit of God." (Revelation 4:5)

"He held seven stars in his right hand." (Revelation 1:16)

"Stars are the angels of seven churches." (Revelation 1:20)

# Philadelphia

"This is the message from the one who is the Amen—the faithful and true witness, the beginning of God's new creation." (Revelation 3:14)

"A white horse was standing there. Its rider was named Faithful and True." (Revelation 19:11)

"He who is the faithful witness to all these things says, 'Yes, I am coming soon!' Amen! Come, Lord Jesus!" (Revelation 22:20)

We can see that the writer is trying to get us to understand that Jesus is the Spirit by assigning all this information to Jesus in the beginning of each letter. Then he ends each letter by telling you the willing one will hear and understand what the Spirit is telling them. God says that if you diligently seek Him that you will find Him (Deuteronomy 4:29). That's why the Bible is the way it is. It's so you will not just read it but devote time to studying it. Then when you use the *entire* Bible to come to your conclusion as to what it says, then you'll have the truth—the whole truth and nothing but the truth. Don't be like the Jehovah's Witnesses, Mormons, Muslims, and many other sects that only use part of the scripture to supposedly confirm their made-up stories. They use scripture out of context or only in part to seemingly make their stories sound true. Read the Bible paragraph by paragraph using the meaning written in that paragraph for what it says, not for what you can make it say. Each paragraph has its own meaning put there by the prophet who wrote it, and that's what you need to take from it. You can take any sentence from any paragraph in any book and fit it into countless stories and fables. But to get the true meaning, you must read it in the context of the paragraph it's in.

Scripture is extremely specific and tells us not to use any outside source other than the Bible itself (Galatians 1:6–10). It says that some were already "following a different way that pretends to be the Good News," and that they were being fooled by people who twist and change the truth. It goes on to say cursed is anyone who preaches a different Christ. It then reiterates that fact. Jude 1:3 says, "God gave this *unchanging truth once for all time* to his holy people" (emphasis mine). Once! Not repeatedly throughout the ages. We already know that God's Word will stand forever (Isaiah 40:8). And we just read that God gave His Word *once* for all time. Is God stupid? What? Would God have to continually give a new, changing Word generation after generation? No! He gave it once! So why did Mohammed for the Muslims, Joseph Smith for the Mormons, Mr. Charles Taze Russell for Jehovah's Witnesses, and countless others believe that they had to bring a new gospel to the world? How could we get the true meaning of the Word that the disciples received from Jesus if God did not make sure that it was passed down unchanged throughout the generations? He did.

Each on of these so-called prophets claim to have been visited by angels or spirits. Maybe they really did see spirits or angels. We have a stern warning in scripture as what to do if this happens. The Bible says, "Dear friends, do not believe everyone who claims to speak by the Spirit. You must test them to see if the spirit they have comes from God. For there are many false prophets in the world." (1 John 4:1) You test them by the Bible that we have today, not the one they want to change it to.

God warned us in a letter to the church of Thyatira not to believe all the false truths out there from Satan but stay strong in the belief that was written once and for all time in the Bible. He said in Revelation 2:24–25:

> "But I also have a message for the rest of you in Thyatira who have not followed this false teaching ('deeper truths,' as they call them—depths of Satan, actually). I will ask nothing more of you except that you hold tightly to what you have until I come."

So many religions out there in the world seem so good and right. Some even do preach good works and good behavior. But if they don't teach you properly about Jesus our Christ and who he really is—God—then they are just sugar-coating the truth and leading you down the wrong path.

None of the religions mentioned here believe that Jesus is God, and we can clearly see from what I've shown you thus far, and will continue showing, that He is just that—God!

# Who Do We Worship?

*L*et's look at who we should worship. We can begin with the Ten Commandments given to us by God himself. The second commandment states, "You must not have any other god but me... You must not bow down to them or worship them, for I, the LORD your God, am a jealous God who will not tolerate your affection for any other gods." (Exodus 20:3 & 5) That counts out Jehovah's Witnesses, who say Jesus is "a god," and then worship Him.

In Acts 12:22–23, King Herod Agrippa accepted worship from the people. They said he had "the voice of a God, not a man!" God sickened him, and he died. God was showing humans not to worship any other. If Jesus is not God, then why did God not sicken and kill Jesus when He accepted worship from the people? There are many instances where people worshipped Jesus in scripture. Here are many times Jesus accepted worship.

| | |
|---|---|
| The wise men came to worship baby Jesus | Deuteronomy 2:2 |
| A man with leprosy worshipped Him | Matthew 8:2 |
| The disciples did when He walked on water | Matthew 14:23 |
| A gentile woman | Matthew 15:25 |
| Mary Magdalene and Jesus's mother after resurrection | Matthew 28:9 |
| A healed man | John 9:38 |
| Angels ordered to worship Him by God | Hebrews 1:6 |
| Disciples after Jesus ascended to heaven | Luke 24:47–53 |

In Revelation 19:10 John says, "I fell down at his feet to worship him, but he said, 'No, don't worship me. I am a servant of God, just like you and other brothers and sisters who testify about their faith in Jesus. Worship only God. For the essence of prophecy is to give a clear witness for Jesus.'" An extraordinarily strong point for this subject is in Luke 4:7–8. Jesus is being tempted by Satan. The devil wants Jesus to worship him. Jesus retorts, "The Scriptures say, 'You must worship the Lord your God and serve only him.'"

Let's put it all together now. In three different books we have it said to worship only God and no other—Matthew 4:10, Deuteronomy 6:13, and Exodus 34:14. We have numerous times in scripture where Jesus was worshipped. In Revelation 5:14, the twenty-four elders and four living beings worshipped God and the Lamb. We already have shown that God shares His glory with no one. Why would Jesus, being tempted by the devil, whom He knows has already been judged and is going to hell, tell him to worship only God and not tell His disciples the same thing when they worshipped Him? Even at the Great Commission in Matthew 28:16–20, they worshipped Him. He's sending them out into the world to spread the gospel. Don't you believe that Jesus made sure they had it correct? He also told them here to baptize people in the name of the Father, the Son, and the Holy Ghost. Proper English would be in the *names* if the three titles were three different beings. But just as Zechariah 14:9 states: "there will be one LORD—his name alone will be worshipped."

In 1 Peter 2:22 it is said that Jesus "never sinned, nor ever deceived anyone." Although some of the disciples were still confused as to whom Christ truly was, Jesus was never confused as to who was to be worshipped. He knew He was God in the flesh, and He was trying to get the disciples to believe it. Thomas was the last to believe. But he finally did and exclaimed, "My Lord and my God!" Hmm. That's what Thomas called Christ—God. I think I'll do the same.

# John the Baptist Prophesied About God

*L*et's look at what John the Baptist says to the Jewish leaders when they question him about who he is. When they ask John if he was the Messiah, he replies in John 1:23 that he is "a voice shouting in the wilderness, 'Clear the way for the LORD's coming!'" He is referencing what the prophet Isaiah said in Isaiah 40:3. He is saying that the Lord that he is preparing the way for is Jesus.

Now let's look at who the Lord was that Isaiah in Old Testament times foresaw. John is quoting Isaiah. In Isaiah 40:3 we read, "Listen! It's the voice of someone shouting, 'clear the way through the wilderness for the LORD! Make a straight highway through the wasteland for our God!'" Isaiah hears John shouting in the wilderness to make a way for Yahweh. The term used here is "LORD," which is translated as YAHWEH, who we know is God. The preface for the New Living Translation states that they consistently used the term "LORD," all capital letters, for

YAHWEH. Isaiah is seeing God Almighty, and John is preparing the way for God's coming. If you read down a little further, Isaiah 40:9 says that "your God is coming." John is preparing the way for Jesus's coming. Isaiah saw what he said was God, and John saw what he said was Jesus. They are the same being. Both prophets are talking about the coming Messiah. Jesus is God here. You have an Old Testament prophet seeing God and a New Testament prophet seeing Jesus in the same instance. Both are talking about the same event. Both see God. Isaiah sees Him as God the Spirit, and John sees Him as God in the flesh as Jesus, but both are God.

## "Ezekiel Prophesying" by Gustave Doré

Eze 1:3 The word of the Lord came expressly unto Ezekiel the priest, the son of Buzi, in the land of the Chaldeans by the river Chebar; and the hand of the Lord was there upon him.

# Names in Ancient Times
# Describe the Person

*L*et's look at the names of people in ancient times. They were given names that meant or described who they were. Unlike today, their names described them. First Samuel 25:25 says, "just as his name suggests." In Isaiah 8:18 we see that names reveal plans the LORD has for His people. Look at the meanings of the following names:

**Satan** means hostile opponent.

**Devil** is slanderer or liar. It says he is the father of lies.

**Abram** is exalted father and was later changed by God to **Abraham**, which means father of many.

**Sarah** means princess.

**Jacob's** name was changed to Israel after he wrestled with God.

**Israel** mean one who struggles with God. Israel is still struggling with God in their disbelief of Jesus.

**Peniel** means face of God. That's what Jacob named the placed he wrestled with God (Genesis 32:1–32 and Hosea 12:3–5).

**Adam** means red earth; his partner **Eve** means life. Adam was literally made from the earth, whereas Eve was made from Adam's rib.

The third son of Ishmael is **Abdel**, which means grief of God.

**Moses** means drawn out (of the river), given to him by the Egyptian woman who found him in a basket floating down the river.

**Molech** is shameful king; the deliberate misvocalization of the name of the pagan god. The consonants for the word *king*—m e l e k—are combined with the vowels for shame—b o s h e t h.

**Daniel** is God is my judge.

**David** is beloved one.

**Isaiah** is Yahweh saves.

**Zion** means citadel.

**Talmud**, which is the Jewish term for the Old Testament, means education or instruction.

**Solomon** is peace, well-being.

**Shadrach,** renamed **Hananiah**, which is Yahweh is gracious.

**Meshach** was renamed **Mishaal**, which is who belongs to God.

**Abednego,** renamed **Azariah,** is Yahweh has helped.

The Bible story says those three were thrown into a fiery furnace by Nebuchadnezzar.

Now we get to **Jesus—Yahweh**—which means saves or Anointed one.

**Immanuel** means God with us, which is a name ascribed to Jesus.

# People Who Say They Saw God

Who were the people in the Old Testament seeing when they said they saw God? Has anyone ever actually seen God? Timothy 6:15–16 states that "no human eye has ever seen God, nor ever will." Exodus 33:20 says that no man shall see God's face and live. Then what was Moses talking about when he said he spoke to God "face to face, as one speaks to a friend?" (Exodus 33:1–23)

Isaiah also said that his eyes have seen the King, the LORD Almighty (Isaiah 6:1–13). Hold your conclusions, there's more.

Look at what Jacob has to say in Genesis 32:22–32. Jacob is wrestling with a bodily figure—a man. He then realizes that he is with God when the figure changes his name to Israel, which means One who Struggles with God. Jacob then names the place where they wrestled Peniel, which means face of God. Jacob says in verse 30, "I have seen God face to face, yet my life has been spared." He was not wrestling a faceless figure—a ghost. He was wrestling a figure that looked like a man, face and all. Who was it? Keep reading.

Ezekiel 1:26–28 describes a figure whose "appearance resembled a man." It does not describe Him vaguely. It's very descriptive in what it says. If He did not have a face it probably would have said so. Neither Moses nor Jacob described faceless figures. Revelation 22:4 says that we will "see His face" at the Second Coming. Job speaks of seeing God's face in his body after his death. He says, "But as for me, I know that my Redeemer lives, and he will stand upon the earth at last. And after my body has decayed, yet in my body I will see God! I will see him for myself. Yes, I will see him with my own eyes. I am overwhelmed at the thought!" (Job 19:25–27)

Zechariah 12:8 says that the Angel of the Lord is God. Look at these other verses on that subject. Read Judges 13:1–25. In verse 11, Manoah asked if He was the man who talked to his wife. He was looking at a figure of a man with a face. Verse 16 points out He is the angel of the LORD. Then down in verse 21 and 22, "Manoah finally realized it was the angel of the LORD, and he said to his wife, 'We will certainly die, for we have seen God!'" Who did they see? Keep reading.

In Genesis 31:11–13, the angel of the Lord says that He is "the God who appeared to you at Bethel." He was speaking of the wrestling match with Jacob and God.

Psalm 89:5–8 lets you know that the heavenly beings—angels—are not as mighty as God. There are many more instances of the angel of the Lord in scripture. I just covered a few here. Let's go on to see who they were looking at.

God has appeared in many ways unto humans throughout history. He appeared as an angel countless times as we have seen previously. He appeared as a fire in the burning bush to Moses and as smoke to guide the wandering Israelites by day and as a fire in the night to guide them. In Job 4:16, God appears as a formless spirit. In Mark 16:9–12, He appears as a man—Jesus—to Mary Magdalene after He arose from the tomb and then appeared in the form of a different man to the two men on the road.

In Daniel 3:25, He appears as the Son of God in the fire with Meshach, Shadrach, and Abednego. The Son of God in the sixth century B.C.? I thought that He was only called the Son of God in the A.D. era. Now we see it specifically said in Philippians 2:6–7. It says that Jesus, "being in the form of God." That's very amazing scripture right there. Then in verse 7 it says that God made Himself into the form of a servant, or a man—Jesus.

In the end times, or the Second Coming of Christ, "we will see him as he really is"—As God! In the form of a man! (1 John 3:2).

Revelation 21:1–27 describes the end times, saying in verse 3 that "God Himself" will live with us.

Adam and Eve really saw a figure walking in the Garden of

Eden with them. "When the cool evening breezes were blowing, the man and his wife heard the LORD God walking about in the garden. So they hid from the LORD God among the trees." (Genesis 3:8)

Are you ready to know who all these people are describing, or have you figured it out already? Turn in your Bible to 2 Corinthians 4:6. It says "For God, who said, 'Let there be light in the darkness,' has made this light shine in our hearts so we could know the glory of God that is seen in the face of Jesus Christ.'" It says that we may know, not assume. They are all seeing what we will all see, God in the last and only form we are able to see—Jesus. We see that "God is spirit" (John 4:24). We see God as we are because "In Christ lives all the fullness of God in a human body." (Colossians 2:9) "For God in all his fulness was pleased to live in Christ." (Colossians 1:19) God Almighty is who they all were seeing, and we will see Him as He truly is if we believe that fact; that is, that we see God in the form of the man Jesus the Christ. Jesus is God.

# Different Figures
# People Say Are God

Over and over in scripture we see these references to different figures that people say are God. Look at John 1:1 where it says, "In the beginning the Word already existed. The Word was with God, and the Word was God." How much plainer does scripture need to be? How do people skirt around straight and simple words such as these, "the Word was God"? This verse with all the evidence I've presented to you here is extremely convincing isn't it?

Hebrews 1:8 says, "To the Son he says, 'your throne, O God, endures forever and ever.'" Here we have God Almighty calling Jesus God. Why would He do that? In the Old Testament, God makes it dramatically clear that He is the only God, there never has been another, and that there never will be another God. It's obviously clear that God wants us to know that point. I'll say it again for Him. There is no other God. So, we have God calling Jesus God because He is. When God says something is true, we can rest assured that He is telling us the true and simple fact—Jesus is God.

In Isaiah 55:11 we see God saying, "It is the same with my word. I send it out, and it always produces fruit. It will accomplish all I want it to, and it will prosper everywhere I send it." Let's break that verse down. God did send out His Word in physical form as Jesus, the Word of God. Remember in Zechariah 2:10–11 where God Almighty sends out God, or Yahweh? Then Jesus says in John 17:5, "bring me into the glory we shared before the world began." God says, "It will accomplish all I want it to," and then Jesus said on the cross, "It is finished" (John 19:30, 4:34). So, God sent out His Word in physical form as Jesus and Jesus finishes God's will. Then God says, "everywhere I send it" in Isaiah. In John 17:18 we see Jesus saying, "Just as you sent me into the world." In John 17:21 we see Jesus state, "so that the world will believe you sent me." Then in John 17:23 we again see Him say, "then the world will know that you sent me." We can determine here that Jesus was sent into the world by God by comparing what is said in the Old Testament to what is recorded in the New Testament.

Don't forget what was said in Zechariah 2:10–11: God Almighty sends Yahweh. Compare that verse with the verse in John 6:29. It says, "Jesus told them, 'This is the only work God wants from you: Believe in the one he has sent.'" The "God" in John is the "God Almighty" in Zechariah. The "one he sent" is

"Jesus" in John, and "Yahweh" in Zechariah, whom we know is God Almighty. So, right here we see Jesus contrasted as Yahweh. They are the same being.

We know that Yahweh is God because Isaiah 45:18 says, "For the LORD is God, he created the heavens and earth." Wasn't Jesus the creator? God speaking to Jesus says, "In the beginning, Lord, you laid the foundation of the earth and made the heavens with your hands." (Hebrews 1:10) Isaiah 42:8 says, "I am the LORD; that is my name!" We know that the Bible translators consistently rendered the name "Yahweh" as "LORD." (preface to the NLT— rendering of divine names)

Put it all into context, and God is God Almighty is Yahweh is LORD is Jesus! And just like Thomas exclaimed in John 20:28: "My Lord and my God!" to Jesus. Jesus is God!

# Verses That Say Jesus Is God

*L*et's look at some scriptures that point-blank say that Jesus is God. Oh yeah, it's in there! Plenty of verses say Jesus is God.

We have already seen the verses in Isaiah 9:6 referring to the Messiah. But let's look at it again. This verse is speaking of one person. It says, "These will be his royal titles: Wonderful Counselor, Mighty God, Everlasting Father, Prince of Peace." Right there in that one verse we have the Father pointed out in the words "Everlasting Father." We have the Son named in the phrase, "Prince of Peace." Then we have the Holy Spirit, "Wonderful Counselor." The fourth title in that verse sums up the first three, "Mighty God." We know that the Messiah is Jesus, and this verse gives Him the titles of the Trinity. He is called the Father, the Son, and the Holy Ghost. The verse then sums it up by calling the Messiah Mighty God. These are all titles of the Messiah that we all know is Jesus. He is called the

Father, the Son, and the Holy Ghost and then summed up with the title Mighty God.

Scripture plainly gives it to us, but some skeptics try to manipulate this like in the Torah (the Jewish Old Testament scriptures). The Jewish translators have changed this verse to read: The Mighty God says his names will be: Counselor, Father, and Prince of Peace. Even though they changed it, it still gives you the three that make up the one. They make it sound like Mighty God is speaking. Not so.

The Dead Sea Scrolls, one of the items dug up in the Middle East that validate Old Testament scripture, date back to just before Christ appeared and have shown us that what is written in the Christian Old Testament has not changed in over two thousand years. It does not read as the Jewish writers have translated it today.

The Dead Sea Scrolls are scrolls that were found starting in 1947 in eleven different caves near the Dead Sea, hence the name, that contained the entire Old Testament in multiple copies. These manuscripts authenticated the entire Old Testament as we read it today. That discovery quieted the howls of a lot of skeptics that boasted that the Bible message has been lost in translation. Jesus quoted out of many books of the Old Testament and the prophets quoted from many more. These papyrus books that were found date back to the time that Jesus walked the earth. That means that the books He was quoting out of are the same ones we are reading today. Jesus quoting from a book gives it the legitimacy it needs to be called authoritative. So, now that it's been proven that we have the same books that Jesus quoted from, shouldn't we have faith in what they say? Yes, we should.

Now look at Jeremiah 23:5–6. Here it's giving a prophecy of the coming King that will reign on the throne of David. We know by scripture that it's Jesus. Verse 6 says about that King: "And this will be his name: 'The LORD Is Our Righteousness.'" That's Yahweh (God). We've already gone over that names describe the person it was given to. The Messiah's name is Yahweh. That's what it says.

We've just seen two places in scripture that says the Messiah is God in the Old Testament. Here's one in the New Testament that is very straightforward. Turn to John 1:1, where we read, "In the beginning the Word already existed. The Word was with God, and the Word was God." How much clearer does the Bible need to be? There is no room for denying what is written. When you take it all together it makes sense. But there are those who change this scripture, namely Jehovah's Witnesses, to read, "the Word was a god." Notice the little "g" in god. We already know that in Isaiah 45:6, Nehemiah 9:6, 1 Kings 8:60, and 2 Samuel 7:22 it says that God is "the" only God. Jehovah's Witnesses even preach that there is but one God but contradict themselves when it comes to this verse. They teach that God and Jesus are two separate beings.

According to them, Jesus was a created being. John 1:3 states that *all* things were created by Him, and nothing exists that He didn't make. It says "nothing." Jesus did not make Himself. He existed since the beginning it says in 1 John 2:13.

Here's one in 1 John 5:20: "And we know that the Son of God has come, and he has given us understanding so that we can know the true God. And now we live in fellowship with the true God because we live in fellowship with his Son, Jesus Christ. He is the only true God, and he is eternal life." We know that Jesus is the life as He says Himself in John 14:6. Scripture adds, "and he is eternal life" after "He is the only true God" so the reader will know who is being talked about. Jesus is God. He is the physical form of the Spirt God.

Daniel 7:9 says, "I watched as thrones were put into place and the Ancient One sat down to judge. His clothing was as white as snow, his hair like purest wool..." This is clearly speaking of God. Now look in Revelation 1:14: "His head and his hair were white like wool, as white as snow." This is referencing Jesus. Why does the Bible consistently describe Jesus in the same manner as it describes God? It's because He is God! How many times do you have to see it to believe it? John 8:24 says, "for unless you believe that I Am who I claim to be, you will die in your sins." Does the Bible have to quote Jesus for it to be from Him? No, it does not! The entire Bible, all sixty-six books, are God's Word. Jesus is the very Word of God. He is called "the author of life." (Acts 3:15) Every word in the Bible is spoken from Jesus. Hebrews 12:2 (KJV) calls Jesus the "author and finisher of our faith." In 1 John 1:1 He is called "the Word of life."

Look in Psalm 102:16. The chapter speaks of the time of the thousand-year reign of Christ starting in verse 12. Verse 16 states that the "LORD," or YHWH, will appear in His glory. All Christians know that what we await is the appearance of Christ in His glory. I believe Christ's Second Coming is at the end of the Tribulation when He comes in His glory to lock Satan away for one thousand years and set up His millennial reign. Matthew 25:31–46, verse 31 in particular, says that "when the Son of Man comes in his glory, and all his angels with him." Revelation 22:7 & 20 both refer to the coming of Jesus.

One last point is in Galatians 3:6–9. Verse 7 says, "The real children of Abraham, then, are those who put their faith in God." Verse 9 says, "So all who put their faith in Christ share the same blessing Abraham received because of his faith." We are told to have faith in God, and just a verse later speaking on the same subject we are told to put our faith in Christ. The Bible just connected God and Christ. If Abraham had to believe in God for his salvation, then why do we have to believe in Jesus for ours? James 2:19 says, "Do you still think it's enough just to believe that there is one God? Well even the demons believe this, and they tremble in terror." And the second commandment instructs us not to worship any other gods besides God. In one verse people are instructed to believe in God, yet in another they are told to believe in Jesus. Is that contradictory? No! That's because Jesus is God. Understood that way, there is never a contradiction in the Bible.

# Conclusion

I am led to conclude that the entire Bible is contradicting itself, it's lost in translation, utterly unbelievable, and we are all doomed. There is no hope for the future of humankind at all—if, and only if, I look at God and Jesus as two separate beings. Nothing at all makes sense when you read scripture with that mind frame. The stories don't flow. They don't make any sense. There is contradiction at every turn of the page. Yet when I look at God and Jesus as one and the same being, as they are, then the scriptures come alive. The entire Bible starts making perfect sense. Page after page, there is unity. The stories in different books talking about the same thing coincide with one another. No contradiction exists. The Bible then makes perfect sense. God knew what He was doing when He was instructing all the prophets what to write and what books he wanted in the Bible when Constantine ordered the Christian leaders to put the Bible scrolls into one book in the 4th century A.D.

When you read the Bible, take each paragraph in its proper context. Don't read too much into the words. Don't reach for hidden meanings or codes. They are just not there. Take each paragraph for what it says. No more, no less. What is written right in front of you is what God wants you to see. Pay attention to what is being said and to whom. Ask the Holy Spirit for guidance, understanding, and knowledge, and read it with the realization and understanding that Jesus is truly our Lord and our God. Then you will get the proper meaning of scripture. If not, you will be lost.

The entire Bible is one continuous story. It is what God wants humankind to know. He tells us how to receive His wonderful gift of salvation. He gives hundreds of years of instances where civilizations followed His teachings and prospered. Once they grew away from His teachings and became too proud and arrogant, they declined. The Bible has a specific subject. It was written with a purpose and a distinct meaning. Take what is written in the Bible for what it says in each paragraph. Do not bring outside meanings into the Bible. Just because a verse out of the Bible sounds good in some other book does not mean it's true in that context. Take the meaning out of scripture; don't put meaning into it. God gives a dire warning against anyone adding to or taking away from His Word.

"And I solemnly declare to everyone who hears the words of prophecy written in this book: If anyone adds anything to what is written here, God will add to that person the plagues described in this book. And if anyone removes any of the words from this book of prophecy, God will remove that person's share in the tree of life and in the holy city that are described in this book" (Revelation 22:18–19).

I feel for all the people out there that have changed the Word of God for their own benefit. God gives such an explicit warning to those who think they need to update scripture. The Bible is extremely specific when it says that it is the unchanging truth given to humans once and for all time in Jude 1:3. Scripture did not have to be repeatedly given to humankind and updated over and over throughout the ages in order for us to have the truth today. God gave it to us one time for all eternity. God is intelligent enough to ensure that His Word would survive throughout time regardless of what humans did. People were out there in the world changing God's Word immediately after it was given, but it remained unchanged and available. In Galatians 1:6–9, the disciples are shocked at how soon the people listened to scripture that had been twisted into wrong doctrine. They give a warning that anyone would be cursed who preached a different word than what they received from them. So, don't be fooled by these false prophets.

Stay strong in your belief.
Keep the Word of God close to your heart.
Endure to the end, and you will be rewarded.
Trust God in all you do.
Jesus is your rock to lean on.
The Holy Spirit is there to comfort you.

You can accept this gift of salvation from God right now and know, not assume, that you will be taken to heaven with Him when He returns. Romans 10:9–10 says, "If you openly declare that Jesus is Lord and believe in your heart that God raised him from the dead, you will be saved. For it is by believing in your heart that you are made right with God, and it is by openly declaring your faith that you are saved." So, right now you can declare to God your faith and belief in Him and His written Word and you *will* be saved.

May God be with you in your daily life, bless you, and welcome you into His eternal kingdom at His glorious Second Coming. Keep reading scripture. You can never get enough of God's Word in your life. Don't be afraid to share your new knowledge of the truth with others, and let the world know that …

# Jesus is God!

### All glory to God above.

### Amen.

Printed in the United States
by Baker & Taylor Publisher Services